Writing Prompts For Middle School

101 Things To Write About For Middle School To Supercharge Their Writing Skills – Writing Prompts For Students

By Subha Malik

Writing Prompts For Middle School

101 Things To Write About For Middle School To Supercharge Their Writing Skills - Writing Prompts For Students

Author: SUBHA MALIK

Printed in the United States Of America
1st printing [August/2017]

ISBN-13: **978-1975983413**

ISBN-10: **1975983416**

WRITING PROMPTS FOR MIDDLE SCHOOL

101 Things To Write About For Middle School To Supercharge Their Writing Skills – Writing Prompts For Students

Introduction:

Best for students "Writing Prompts For Middle School" is an interesting and inspiring activity journal with over 100 thought provoking things to write about.

Writing Prompts For Middle School is aimed to make your writing process easier by offering over 100 writing situations.

This writing journal will help students to pull in their prior knowledge and personal experiences to write about topics that interest them.

If you are a parent and looking for writing ideas for your kids you will be amazed to know that you will no longer fight for writing ideas for your middle school kids. In this journal you will find a lot of inspiring, fun questions and writing prompts all aimed at journal writing for middle school.

This journal is crafted in such a way to get students think in a new and refreshing way and it also lets them gain a deeper understanding of their inner self while having fun.

On the whole, the questions and writing prompts within this unique journal are meant to provide students with a simple yet integrative pastime.

DEDICATION

This Book Is Dedicated to All The Middle School Students and Their Inner Kids.

I also dedicate this effort to My Parents, My Beloved Wife and My Three Little Angels!

ACKNOWLEDGMENTS

I would like to express my gratitude to all wonderful people who played a vital role throughout my life like my parents, my teachers, my mentors and my friends. I would not be able to create this Book and many others without their loyal support.

Especially I would like to thank my wife and rest of my family, who supported and encouraged me in spite of not giving them enough time.

ABOUT THE AUTHOR

Subha Malik is a blogger, writer and author, he loves to write about self help topics and his aim is to inspire people and help them live better lives.

You can check out his other books here:

amazon.com/author/subhamalik

Visit His Blog: www.storeinspire.com

Paste a photo to your notebook page and write about it

Write about the world 50 years from now, what people will eat, what they will believe?

Write a short story about a new creature (Vampire goat, Zombie Lobster, Clown shark)

What if you have a robot servant? How will it look? What would you ask him to do for you and what features it would have?

Describe your very first memory

Write about your name: what does it mean? Do you like your name?

What if you can invent something new? What features it will have? And what problems it will solve?

Write five sentences that start with the words “I love to...”

Write down names of 10 countries in the world that you most like to visit

Write about a road trip you took recently

Write about the world without any electricity, water and gas. How people's life will change and what they would do to survive?

Write about a day when you did some act of kindness

Where would you like to live in, a tree house or a rainforest and why?

Write about your best ever family vacation memory

Write about you becoming a character in your favorite video game or movie

List ten items in your bucket list for the next five years

Write a story starting with "An alien comes to Earth, and...

Who is your family legend, tell a story about him

What would you do, if all
your wishes come true?

What does honesty means to you? Is it important to be honest?

Write about benefits of exercising? Do you think exercise is necessary at the age you are now?

How important it is to have good manners? Why?

What if you were a kite?

Tell a story about a field trip your class took

What are you afraid of?

What do colors means to you? What you think colors are like?

Write about your favorite book this year· Also write what makes it your favorite?

I have decided to...

Write about things you want to do this weekend

Tell a story about your first day at school

What are 5 great things about you?

What bugs you most?

What color is the water?

What if there were no cars, bikes, buses, trains, boats or planes? How our lives would change?

I learnt from someone how to...

Life is full of...

Tell a story about visiting a very dark house

Write about your favorite legend in the history

List 5 places in the world you would like to live in

Write about your best weekend and what made it so special?

My dream vacation is...

I helped my mother by...

Tell a story about your most exciting day at school

I love to collect...

Write about a windy day you ever had

Make a list of things you think this world needs now?

Write about your plans for tomorrow

My favorite day of week is...

Write about your feelings when you do something wrong

Do you think school is fun?
Why?

What if you got a present you don't like?

What do you think about birds?

My favorite month is.........because......

Make a list of things which make you happy

If you get some extra money for you allowance, what would you do with it?

What is your favorite character from your book and why?

Tell about the day when you failed to do your homework

What if you found a lot of diamonds in your backyard?

Oh, no, it is raining and I can't...

You're going on a world tour and you can only take three people with you, who would you take with and why?

What would you do, if you were a snowflake?

Tell about the time when you helped your father

If I could have wings, I would fly to...

What your teachers say about you in your absence?

Tell a story about the day you got your first pet

Tell a story about something unexpected happened to you

Write about time when you felt truly frightened

List 5 things which are on your wish-list right now

Write about an unforgettable thing ever happened to you

Tell something special about your classroom

What puts you in a bad mood?

Tell me about your favorite teacher, what makes him/her so likeable

Who would be the only person if you could invite over your house?

Make List of 10 things you plan to do this year

Tell me how you make friends

I am really good at........

What you feel about your current height and how tall you want to be?

Write a poem about winter

Write names of five junk foods you know

Do you love sunshine, what does it make you to feel like?

Do you have to follow some rules at home? What are those rules?

What you do when someone teases you?

What would you do if you happen to be President of USA for one day?

Tell a story about a dark cave

What if the world were made of chocolate?

What are your favorite places to play?

What you think about math?
Are you good at math?

Write about time when you felt like crying?

Write about your bedroom...

Tell a story about a day when you felt very lucky

How many people you have in your family, write about each person

What is your favorite color?
Also write names of things
that are that color

Do you love spring or fall?
Write about the season you
love the most

Write poem by using the words: water, rain, raindrops, and rainbow

What do you love to hear and from whom?

Write about your most special day in life. Also tell what made it special to you?

Tell a story about a dangerous experience

Write about the difficult decision that you had to make

What makes you feel sorry for and why?

What do you do when you can't sleep?

What do you do when people misunderstand you?

Leave a Review
If you enjoyed this Book, please don't forget to leave a review about this Book on Amazon! This way others can enjoy this too!

I'm just a home based author with NO "big marketing company" behind me, so I highly appreciate your review, and it only takes a minute to do.

To Submit a Review:

1. Just go to Amazon and under the BOOKS category, search this Book's title;

[WRITING PROMPTS FOR MIDDLE SCHOOL: 101 Things to Write about for Middle School to Supercharge Their Writing Skills***]*** to get to the product detail page for this eBook on Amazon.

2. Click **Write a customer review** in the Customer Reviews section.

3. Click Submit.
Thank you in advance for submitting!"

The End…

Thanks For Buying My Book

CPSIA information can be obtained
at www.ICGtesting.com
Printed in the USA
BVHW030341091218
535138BV00001B/113/P